Dropping In On...
FRANCE

Philip Bader

A Geography Series

THE ROURKE BOOK COMPANY, INC.
VERO BEACH, FLORIDA 32964

Printed in the United States of America

**Library of Congress
Cataloging-in-Publication Data**

Bader, Philip, 1969-
 France / Philip Bader.
   p. cm. — (Dropping in on)
 Includes index.
 Summary: Briefly describes some of the regions and notable features of France.
 ISBN 1-55916-280-5
 1. France—Juvenile literature. [1. France.] I. Title. II. Series.

DC17 .B23 2000
944—dc21

00-023924

Printed in the USA

France

Official Name: French Republic

Area: 211,208 square miles (547,029 square kilometers)

Population: 58.6 million

Capital: Paris

Largest City: Paris

Highest Elevation: Mont Blanc, 15,781 feet (4,810 meters)

Official Language: French

Major Religion: Roman Catholic (81%)

Money: French franc

Form of Government: Constitutional Republic

Flag:

TABLE OF CONTENTS

Our Blue Ball — The Earth

The Earth can be divided into two hemispheres. The word hemisphere means "half a ball"—in this case, the ball is the Earth.

The equator is an imaginary line that runs around the middle of the Earth. It separates the Northern Hemisphere from the Southern Hemisphere. North America— where Canada, the United States, and Mexico are located—is in the Northern Hemisphere.

The Northern Hemisphere

When the North Pole is tilted toward the sun, the sun's most powerful rays strike the northern half of the Earth and less sunshine hits the Southern Hemisphere. That is when people in the Northern Hemisphere enjoy summer. When the

North Pole is tilted away from the sun and the Southern Hemisphere receives the most sunshine, the seasons reverse. Then winter comes to the Northern Hemisphere. Seasons in the Northern Hemisphere and the Southern Hemisphere are always opposite.

Get Ready for France

Let's take a trip! Climb into your hot-air balloon, and we'll drop in on a country located at the western edge of Europe. France is bordered by oceans on three sides to the north and west. On three other sides, mountains separate France from the countries of Belgium, Germany, Switzerland, Italy, and Spain. The island of Corsica, located off the southeastern coast in the Mediterranean Sea, also belongs to France.

The center of France is mostly flat, with the exception of a rocky *plateau* called the Massif Central. These old mountains were once volcanoes. Wind and water have flattened their peaks and created caves and strange rock formations.

France is divided into twenty-two regions. Culture, history, and language can differ greatly from region to region. Yearly festivals provide an opportunity to celebrate these differences in clothing, music, language, and food.

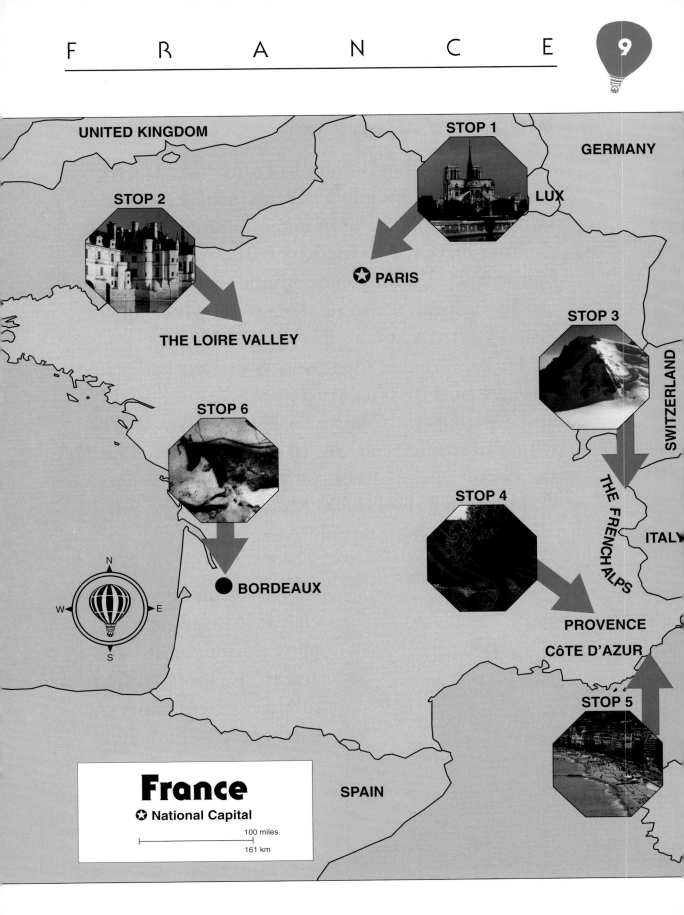

Stop 1: Paris

Paris is the largest city in France and the capital of the country. People from the north called Celts built the city 2,000 years ago on a small island in the middle of the Seine River. Today, the Cathedral of Notre Dame stands on this island and the French call it the Île de la Cité, which means "Island of the City."

Paris is divided into twenty districts called *arrondissements*. This word means "rounding off" and describes these sections of the city well: They wind out from the center like a snail shell. Through the center of the city runs the Seine River. Famous buildings like the Louvre Museum and the Eiffel Tower are built along the river's banks.

The Métro subway train runs underneath the city. It stops in many places throughout Paris and in the more modern suburbs, where many of the people in Paris live.

Notre Dame Cathedral sits on a small island in the Seine River, called the Île de la Cité.

*Now let's fly **southwest** to the Loire Valley.*

The Eiffel Tower

A French engineer named Gustav Eiffel built the Eiffel Tower in 1889 to celebrate the 100th anniversary of the French Revolution. He used 7,000 tons of iron to make this tower, and it stands 984 feet (300 meters) tall. Gustav Eiffel also helped design the Statue of Liberty.

Many people in Paris at that time did not like the Eiffel Tower because it looked different from any other building in the city. Today, it has become a favorite tourist site and one of the best-known monuments in the world.

The Eiffel Tower has two platforms where people can stand and look over the center of Paris. Powerful elevators also take visitors to a third platform at the top of the tower. From here, the view of the city is clear for many miles.

Every seven years, city workers paint the Eiffel Tower using 50 tons of paint. At night, bright lights shine on it and make it visible from all over the city.

The Eiffel Tower offers visitors a panoramic view of Paris and its surrounding countryside.

The Château de Chenanceaux, called Château des Dames (Castle of Women), spans the width of the Cher River.

A view of the château at Versailles from one of its many flower gardens.

Stop 2: The Loire Valley

To the south and west of Paris, the Loire River winds gently through the hills of the Loire Valley on its way to the Atlantic Ocean. During the Middle Ages, France fought many wars with England to keep control over this region.

French rulers built large castles called *châteaux* along the banks of the river and in the hills above it to defend the valley against invaders. It was here that a fourteen-year-old girl, Joan of Arc, led the French armies to victory against the English. Vineyards that stretch across this valley produce some of France's finest wines.

The largest château in France is located outside the Loire Valley. In 1623, King Louis the Thirteenth built a small hunting lodge at a place called Versailles. Over the next 150 years, the kings who followed him transformed this small lodge into the largest and most elegant royal palace in Europe.

Now let's fly **southeast** *to The French Alps.*

English Channel

1

2 Loire Valley

Atlantic Ocean

N
W E
S

Mediterranean Sea

Stop 3: The French Alps

Moving southeast from the central valleys, the land rises sharply in a series of towering mountain peaks called the French Alps. These mountains run along the eastern border of France. Mont Blanc, one of the peaks on the French-Italian border, rises 15,781 feet (4,810 meters). It is the highest peak in Europe.

At the base of Mont Blanc is the resort village of Chamonix. The first Winter Olympic Games were held here in 1924. Skiers from all over the world visit this region to test their skill on the surrounding ski slopes.

The city of Grenoble is located in the Dauphiné region of France near the western edge of the Alpine mountains. Surrounded by natural parks and beautiful views of the Alps, Grenoble is a modern city with tall skyscrapers and a nuclear research plant. The Musée de Grenoble is the second largest museum in France.

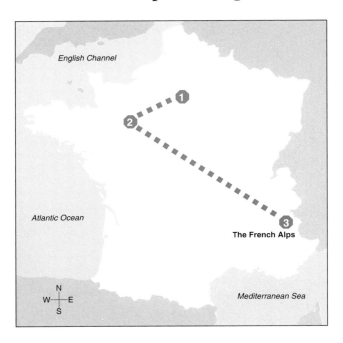

English Channel

Atlantic Ocean

The French Alps

Mediterranean Sea

N
W E
S

The snowy peak of Mont Blanc, near Chamonix, France, is the tallest in Western Europe.

 *Now let's fly **south** to Provence.*

Growing Up in France

Children in France attend school from the ages of six to fifteen. The school year begins in September and runs until the end of June. Students attend the *école*, or elementary school, until the age of eleven. Then, they begin high school in the *lycée*. After high school, students take a test called the *baccalauréat* if they want to go to college.

Families in large cities like Paris often live in apartments because houses are expensive and space is limited. In smaller villages, some children might grow up on a vineyard where they would help with the grape harvests each year.

The people of France come from many different ethnic groups, including African, Asian, and Northern European. Children in France are likely to go to a Catholic church, because more than 80 percent of French people are Roman Catholics. However, other French children grow up in homes where Islam, Judaism, or another religion may be traditional.

Children play with toy sailboats in the Tuileries garden at the Louvre.

Children at recess in Orleans, France.

Stop 4: Provence

In the south of France, the Provence region combines many different kinds of geography. Rocky cliffs rise up from the Mediterranean Sea. Further inland, rolling hills and the Alpilles mountains cover most of the region.

The Romans lived here more than 2,000 years ago, and they called it *Provincia*. Two Roman arenas still stand in the cities of Nîmes and Arles.

The French love Provence for its colorful scenery and bright sunlight. For most of the year, the climate is mild. In the winter months, an icy wind called the *mistral* (which means "meteor") blows out of the north along the Rhône River.

The Provence region is a popular spot for those who want to escape the cares of city life. Its medieval villages, fields of purple lavender, and groves of cypress and olive trees have inspired some of France's most celebrated artists.

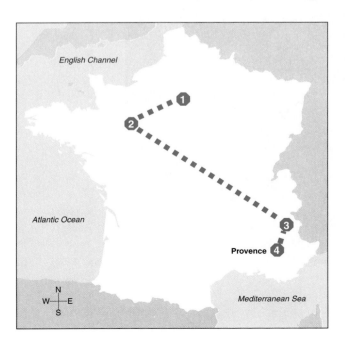

Now let's fly **southeast** to Côte d'Azur.

Above: The colorful landscapes of Provence, like this field of lavender, inspired many of France's greatest artists.

Right: A falcon handler entertains children during a festival at the Château de Beaucaire in Provence.

The Impressionists

In the late nineteenth century, a group of artists in Paris decided to try a new way of painting. They used bright colors and thick brushstrokes to show how different kinds of light changed the way a mountain or a building looked.

This group of artists did not have much success at first. One critic gave them the nickname Impressionists because their paintings did not seem to show actual objects, only "impressions" of them. The nickname stuck, and today Impressionist paintings are among the most famous and valuable works of art in the world.

The Impressionists found inspiration for their paintings in the villages and people of rural France. One Postimpressionist, Vincent van Gogh, lived in the village of Arles. He completed many paintings while he lived there. One of the most famous is a picture of the room where he lived in Arles. The Impressionist Paul Cézanne was born in the village of Aix-in-Provence. He painted dozens of pictures of a nearby mountain called Mont Sainte-Victoire.

Above: The Artist's Bedroom at Arles *by Vincent van Gogh.*

Below: One of the Mont Sainte-Victoire *paintings by Paul Cezanne.*

Stop 5: Côte d'Azur

Moving south from the high peaks of the French Alps, the land sweeps down to the bright blue waters of the Mediterranean Sea. The Côte d'Azur, meaning "Blue Coast," attracts millions of visitors each year because of its warm climate and popular resort cities.

In the city of Cannes, movie stars gather each summer for the Cannes Film Festival. Hotels, shops, and private beaches line the waterfront boulevard. Above the coast, narrow, winding streets cut through the hills of the oldest part of the city.

To the east of Cannes is the city of Nice. More than 150 years ago, English nobles flocked to Nice to escape the cold northern winters. Nice still attracts tourists to its beaches and its historic section.

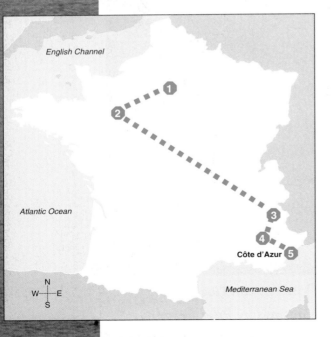

English Channel

Atlantic Ocean

Côte d'Azur 5

Mediterranean Sea

N
W E
S

Now let's fly **west** to Bordeaux.

The waterfront at Nice, France.

Stop 6: Bordeaux

The city of Bordeaux sits on the left bank of the Garonne River in the Aquitaine region of southwestern France. To the north, the river meets an *estuary* called the Gironde. This estuary cuts inland from the Atlantic Ocean.

Bordeaux has been a center of wine production for more than 1,000 years, and the city is surrounded by vineyards. In the center of Bordeaux are old mansions and wide city squares built during the eighteenth century by some of France's most famous architects.

The history of the Aquitaine region dates back to prehistoric times. In caves located east of Bordeaux, scientists have found ancient paintings of buffalo, horses, and reindeer. Many believe that these paintings are more than 20,000 years old and that they were painted by Cro-Magnon men and women who lived in the caves.

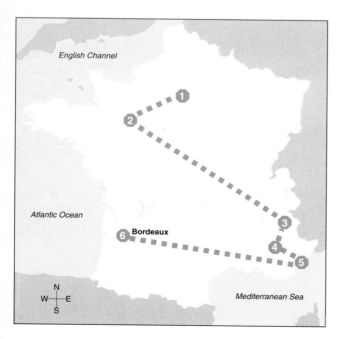

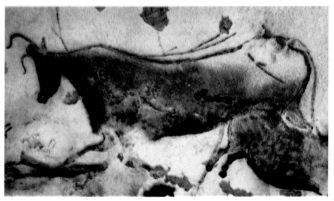

Above: The Monument des Girondins, located in the Esplanade de Quinconces in Bordeaux.

Right: An example of the cave paintings discovered in a cave in Lascaux, near Bordeaux.

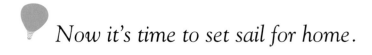

Now it's time to set sail for home.

The Foods of France

The French like to buy their food fresh each day. Some people shop at large supermarkets, but many prefer to visit the smaller shops that specialize in certain kinds of food like the *pâtisserie* (pastry shop) or the *boucherie* (butcher). Outdoor markets called *marchées* sell fresh vegetables, fish, breads, cheeses, and other foods.

Breakfast in France might include a fresh pastry called a *croissant* served with butter and jelly, a strong cup of coffee or a mug of hot chocolate. Lunch is usually the largest meal of the day. It can have as many as six different courses including a main course of meat, salad, vegetables, fruit, and cheese.

Common dinner menus might feature a fish soup called *bouillabaisse. Bœuf bourguignonne* is a stew made with beef, red wine, and vegetables. Other popular dishes are *coq au vin* (chicken cooked in red wine), *foie gras* (a paste made of goose livers with truffles and herbs), *quiche* (a pie made with egg custard, cheese, and ham or spinach), *crêpes* (thin pancakes stuffed with fruit or meat), and seafoods like oysters, shellfish, and eels.

Above: Hundreds of different cheeses are produced throughout France.

Right: Crêpes are a favorite dish throughout France, and each region has its own method of preparing them.

Glossary

arrondissement   One of the twenty districts of Paris.

baccalauréat   A diploma that French children receive after completing secondary school.

châteaux   Large castles built long ago to protect the French from invaders.

estuary   A water passage where an ocean tide meets a river current.

Impressionists   A school of French painters who painted their "impressions" of a scene instead of realistic images.

marchée   An outdoor market where people buy fresh vegetables, meats, breads, and cheeses.

mistral   A cold winter wind that blows along the Rhône River.

musée   A museum.

plateau   A large, relatively flat area of land that is much higher than the land next to it.

Further Reading

Axworthy, Ann, and Anni Axworthy. *Anni's Diary of France*. New York: Whispering Coyote Press, 1992.

Munro, Roxie. *The Inside-Outside Book of Paris*. New York: Dutton Children's Books, 1992.

Sturges, Jo. *Discovering France*. New York: Crestwood House, 1993.

Tomlins, James. *We Live in France*. New York: The Bookwright Press, 1983.

Suggested Web Sites

French Travel Gallery
<http://www.europe-france.com>

Paris Guide
<http://www.smartweb.fr/louvre>

Vive la France
<http://www.vive-la-france.org>

Index

Acknowledgments and Photo Credits
Cover: © PhotoDisc, Inc.; pp. 11, 13, 14, 21, 24-25: © PhotoDisc, Inc.; pp. 14 (Versailles),
19: © Ulrike Welsch; pp. 17, 23, 27, 29 (crêpes): © 1999 Corbis; pg. 19: R. Kent Rasmussen;
pg. 21: © Nik Wheeler; pg. 29: Fred Slavin/French Gov't Tourist Office.
Maps: Moritz Design.